Broken Things

and other tales

First published 2020 by The Hedgehog Poetry Press

Published in the UK by
The Hedgehog Poetry Press
5, Coppack House
Churchill Avenue
Clevedon
BS21 6QW

www.hedgehogpress.co.uk

ISBN: 978-1-913499-03-7

A CIP Catalogue record for this book is available from the British Library.

Contents

Broken Things	7
The Heron	8
feathers	9
Winter Solstice	10
Half-light	11
Vernal Equinox	12
Dusk	13
Night	14
Lauds	15
The Road	16
Labyrinth	17
The Giants and The Birds	18
Secrets	19
What Comes From Silence	20
nourish	21

Broken Things

and other tales

by

Vicky Allen

BROKEN THINGS

Walk any path
in any direction
around the old field fringes
across the wide wild beaches
and there are traces,
for those who look,
of ones who came before

I have collected traces
as I go, walking any path,
broken bits of cups and plates
blue and white fragments of forgotten meals
fractured from their whole
and turned over in the soil
sown for some later renewal

I turn over these broken things now
with curious fingers
wondering how they came to be lost
and found.
Was this once a plate, a cup,
 a common meal passed between friends?
The everyday mystery of the forgotten

Any path
in any direction
leads to broken things
blue and white memories
trodden down beneath careless feet
but beauty breaks the dirt
and brokenness becomes shared

THE HERON

she stands
folded
silent
still

grey ghost
watcher
metal and stone
meets
feather, bone

waiting
bridging
this sold
world
and
its paler cousin

she shall always stand
folded
silent
still

she will always know
stillness
brings nourishment
in time

FEATHERS

falling like manna
soft
kissing grasses, moss
with careful fingers
I gather them

one by one
each
held to mutable light
is a universe of change
too vast to relinquish

until all adds up
to a weight of possibility
impossible to carry
the proverbial ton
does not relent

mindful of daily manna
spoiling past its span
today I carry
one single feather
it is enough

WINTER SOLSTICE

I stretch out into
the generous space of the longest night
it is like
the heavy eiderdown
from my grandmother's spare bed
or like
a soothing hand
upon my crumpled brow
the winter
balances delicately upon tonight
the length of it
measured by stars and moons and tides
I stretch out
every part of me glad for the heavy solace of night
morning comes
the year turns
and I stretch into the light

HALF-LIGHT

the light is halfway here
solstice and equinox
thread a slender ribbon
between winter and spring
and in the half-light
all I know for certain
is the darkness cannot quite forget
how the flower turns to the light

VERNAL EQUINOX

With sudden fanfare
spring's sharply opened curtains
are a longed-for surprise
the light streams in
the dark scatters.

Even-handed
day and night spread
celestial balance
the vernal welcome mat
an open door to coming days.

Lion and lamb
are quiet today
a truce
their faces turning
to the March sun.

DUSK

the day is dulling down to dusk
cold sharpens its knives
a buzzard faintly cries
my breath catches

cold sharpens its knives
and somewhere between wonder and peace
my breath catches
I listen, I watch

somewhere between wonder and peace
a buzzard faintly cries
I listen, I watch
the day is dulling down to dusk

NIGHT

I need the night
blessing and balm
of the softening sky
as the day folds its hands, finished

the soothing weight
across scratchy eyes
a mother's hand, resting
sounds still to reverent hush

velvety animal-black with
trails of stars summoning silence
moon cycles moving heaven and earth
to bring sleep

I need the night
long, dream-hazed, quiet.
how else to welcome another dawn?

LAUDS

solitary bird
sings liquid light and honey
calling morning forth
fracturing the dark sky

tiny, immovable command
a wakening
a holy summoning
from pre-dawn hush

cocooned from wakefulness
the dark my shield
I hear her song
and turn from it, unready

light breaches
my defences
the squabble of birdsong
brings the inevitable day

THE ROAD

The silver sliver of road
stretches taut
cold and aching.
The road and I
we are both worn away
by each endless trip.
But there is no end
that I want to come

LABYRINTH

At the beating heart
of the hospital
the labyrinth path pulses
only to you
with small steps
with wide eyes

Corridor clattering
rattling
a parallel universe
of life
wide purpose
small routines

In here
we are held
by the holding of your hand
the circling world fades
in the small space
outside wide time

We are at the heart
of the labyrinth
and we are stilled
the wide world retreats
and we become small together
here I stay
and then

you go

THE GIANTS AND THE BIRDS

(First published in "Bridges Not Walls" Dove Tales anthology 2019)

There was once a wall between the world and itself
and giants threw stones
across the divide
that landed in their own backyard
the sky was divided between the world and itself
and birds might only land wherever there was an olive branch
so they flew forever, hurting for home

There once was a wall between the world and itself
and in the final desperate days
the giants and the birds
wearily wondered about other things
like: making a doorway in the wall, pathways to the world
like: planting olive trees, making a garden
and the world turned, finally finding a way home

SECRETS

winter marsh
stores her secrets
silent
blank-faced
empty

when ice cracks
her barren pools
and north winds
scour
scrape

it is my quiet delight
remembering how
spring's succulent jewels
hide
wait

for I have my secrets too

WHAT COMES FROM SILENCE

(with thanks to Wendell Berry)

I sat long
the bleached and broken branch
sacred as any stiff-backed pew

stillness was learned
as dusk became
a gauzy sky-robe of constellations

I expected silence
to be peace
some sort of hard-earned joy

but instead I wept
as silence offered me
my own star-shrouded heart

NOURISH

grain
air
water
yeast
wait, wait, wait
kneading, kneading
wait
the slow and slowing rise

I am nourished
by
the baking of
this slow and sacred bread
and
I am nourished

by slow
by grain
by air
by water
by yeast
by wait
by wait
by every blessed thing

Acknowledgements

Thank you to everyone in my wonderful writers' group in Edinburgh. You are a true community of encouragers and consistently cheer me on to do more than I could have imagined was possible. I am so grateful for you all.

Special thanks go to the wonderful community around Songs That Wonder, who first listened to me read many of these poems. It was truly a sacred space for so many of us and I will miss you all.

I am so thankful for all my friends who have been such true (and patient!) encouragers for many years. There are too many of you to mention but particular thanks go to Emma & Jon, to Laurie, to Heather, to Keith & Donna, and of course to amazing photographers (who made my artwork look 100% better) and all-round people of awesomeness Niels & Alie.

Mark at Hedgehog Poetry Press - I am so very grateful for this lovely opportunity and all your hard work and patience.

Thank you to my lovely extended family for supporting and encouraging me for so long.

Love and gratitude in every possible way to Brian, Eve and Caleb who are my favourite fellow adventurers.

About Vicky Allen

Vicky Allen lives on the south east coast of Scotland. The land, seascapes and rich heritage of story and folklore in Scotland are influential in her poetry.

Recent anthology "Reaching For Mercy" (Proost 2018) features her work, as does the 2019 Dove Tales anthology "Bridges Not Walls" and children's poetry anthology "Are We In A Book" (Black Agnes Press 2019). She performed her spoken-word show "Wonder Lines" for the 2018 Edinburgh Book Fringe, with further performances taking place in 2019. She regularly participates in open mic and community poetry events. She has work published online and in print with Mslexia, Vox Poetica, The Writers Cafe, Bonnie's Crew and the Scottish Centre for Geopoetics journal "Stravaig" amongst others. Vicky was the 2018 Faith/Unbelief poetry slam winner.

"Broken Things" is Vicky's first poetry pamphlet.

"With the eyes of a watcher and the pen of a mystic Vicky Allen causes us to slow down and take notice of the world around. Those things we do not see in the rush of our lives. Her words take us into that place where the visible world around us meets the invisible world inside us and somewhere in that confluence our very being in this world is renewed and transformed."

- Joel Mckerrow- Writer, Speaker, Poet, Artist Ambassador for TEAR Australia ~

"Like the Heron in her poem of that name, Vicky Allen takes the time to enquire beneath the fluid surface of her subjects, rewarding us with a clear voiced, finely distilled collection of poems."

- Martin Daws, Spoken Word Poet, Creative Educator, author of "Geiriau Gogs" and "Skintight the Sidewalk". Young People's Laureate Wales (2013-16)

"I love Vicky's poetry and it's been a real honour to be able to collaborate with her in the past.

Vicky is a unique mix of storyteller and poet. Her poems hold together rhythmically yet also have the feel of epic stories with deep meaning and playful humour. She performs with a smile and is able to create those wonderful deep moments of silence when everyone engages with her words and rhymes."

- Andy Freeman, writer, poet, founder & co-director of Space to Breathe

"Words arise in all of us, but only a special few can allow themselves to be shaped by them. Vicky is one of those who do. Her words weave rich stories and images that swirl about us then lead us in her direction."

- Chris Goan, poet

"Vicky's poems, at once delicate and robust, earthy and ethereal, transport her listener/reader right to their windswept locales, and indirectly to her heart. On one of her lonesome starry nights or jagged sand paths is where even the cynic can find himself disarmed, nodding reflexively in understanding to faith, longing and wonder."

- Rachel Zylstra, singer - songwriter